Civil Procedure Outline
Elite law school notes

Kevin Lomax, JD

Copyright © 2020 Kevin Lomax

All rights reserved. This book or any portion thereof may not be reproduced or used in any manner whatsoever without the express written permission of the publisher.

Disclaimer: This book does not in any way establish or recommend any legal guidelines or legal practice. The information presented in this book is solely intended to be used for exam preparation and not for representing clients. I take no responsibility for any errors you may make using the information presented in this book.

Preface

I wrote this outline when I was a student at a top ten law school. I spent over 100 hours working on it, in fact, perfecting it. I used it to ace the class, and in the process learned to study smarter, not harder. Use this outline, in addition to reading the cases assigned to you, with an emphasis on *really* knowing this outline come exam time. I am confident with this outline you too now have the tool to ace your class!

I. **WHERE CAN THE SUIT BE BROUGHT?**
   1. Subject Matter Jurisdiction – Whether a court can hear a particular type of dispute. S.M.J cannot be conferred by the parties if it has not been granted by Congress
   2. Courts of general jurisdiction – can hear any kind of claim between any persons unless there is legal authority saying they cannot hear a particular kind of case
   3. Courts of limited jurisdiction – Can hear only those cases that are specifically authorized by the statutes that set up the particular court
      - Federal Courts are only courts of limited jurisdiction
      - Congress decides the precise subject matter jurisdiction of the federal courts:
         28 U.S.C. §1331 – Authorizes jurisdiction over matters involving a federal question
         28 U.S.C. §1332 – <u>DIVERSITY JURISDICTION</u>: authorizes jurisdiction over disputes where no plaintiff is a citizen of the same state as a defendant and the amount in controversy exceeds the sum of $75k. <u>Citizenship</u>-depends on residency and an intent to remain indefinitely.
   4. Personal Jurisdiction – The state or federal court in the state must have power to render a judgment against the defendant.
   5. Venue
      - The place where judicial authority may be exercised and is intended for the convenience of the litigants
   6. Venue vs. Jurisdiction
      - The most important difference between Venue and Jurisdiction is that a party may consent to be sued in a district that otherwise would be an improper venue, and it waives its objection to venue if it fails to assert it promptly
      - Jurisdiction is the power to adjudicate
      - If all the defendants reside in a single state, venue can be claimed either in any district in which any defendant resides or in a district in which a substantial part of the events occurred
      - If all defendants do not reside in a single state, venue must be put where the events occurred

II. **PLEADINGS**
   a. Purposes of Pleadings
      i. Give the court and the adversary fair notice of the pleader's contentions
      ii. State the facts each party believes to exist
      iii. Narrow the issues
      iv. Provide a means for speeding disposition of sham claims and unsubstantial defenses
      v. Notice Pleading: little need for detail in the pleadings. Contrast with fact pleading and issue pleading
      vi. Steps in Pleading Stage: P's complaint, D's response in the form of motions and/or answer, and rather rarely P's motions and/or reply

b. Lawyer's Responsibility
   i. <u>FRCP 11:</u> imposes an obligation on counsel and client to stop, think, investigate and research before filing papers either to initiate the suit or to conduct the litigation. Doesn't apply to discovery, appeal
   ii. Triggered by signing
   iii. Required: Reasonable basis for claim + Reasonable investigation
   iv. Opposing party has 21 days to correct its mistakes
   v. Plead on information and belief; don't need to go to discovery to get enough relevant information to base a claim. 11(b)
   vi. Want to prevent collateral litigation = litigation about litigation
   vii. Sanctions can be brought about in two ways:
      1. Motion – Can shift attorney's fees
      2. Judge – Show cause order is issued, which means that the plaintiff must show why he hasn't violated Rule 11; judge can't impose monetary sanctions, but he has plenary power
c. The Complaint – the allegations or "declarations" in a complaint must be sufficiently detailed or specific so that the defendant is afforded a fair opportunity to formulate an appropriate response.
   <u>FRCP 8(a)</u> stipulates that a claim for relief contain:
      1. Grounds of the court's jurisdiction regarding the claim
      2. A short and plain statement of the claim showing that the pleader is entitled to relief
      3. A demand for judgment for the relief P seeks
      4. Complaint can't be baldly conclusory
      5. At the pleading stage a party may plead inconsistent versions of the facts because there is no apparent reason for the party to know which version is true. A statement constituting an admission in one count is not viable or incorporated into other counts
d. The Complaint: Burdens
      1. Burden of Pleading – one must allege that element of the claim or defense; one cannot expect the other party to do so
      2. Burden of Production – at trial one must produce evidence that tend to demonstrate the proposition at stake, i.e., a *reasonable inference* can be drawn from the evidence more probably than not.
      3. Burden of Persuasion – In a civil case means that one must persuade the trier of fact that one's version of facts *is more likely* than not to be true
e. The Complaint: Motions <u>FRCP 7(b)</u>
   i. A motion is a request to the court for an order
   ii. Any D who wishes to raise any defenses or objections permitted in Rule 12 must do so *before* filing an answer. A P who wishes to raise Rule 12 objections or defenses to a counterclaim must do so prior to filing a reply to the counterclaim. <u>FRCP 12(b)</u>
   iii. Consists of 4 different documents (may be combined into one):
      1. Motion itself – a request for the specific relief sought

2. Notice of motion – tells the opposing party when the motion will be heard
3. Affidavit - setting forth any factual information necessary for granting the motion
4. Memorandum of law – explaining, with reference to supporting authorities, the legal basis for the motion
f. Defendant Responses; Listed under FRCP 12(b)
    a. *Pre-Answer* Motions
        i. Lack of personal jurisdiction FRCP 12(b)(2), improper venue FRCP 12(b)(3), insufficient process FRCP 12(b)(4), and insufficient service of process FRCP 12(b)(5). Must include in initial motion or answer, whichever of the two comes first, or an amended pleading. The failure to raise these defenses constitutes a waiver of these objections FRCP 12(g) and (h). 12(g) requires one to include in the pre-answer motion all 12(b) defenses "then available" to one
        ii. Lack of subject matter jurisdiction FRCP 12(b)(1) is a non-waivable defense. Objections to the court's subject matter jurisdiction may be raised prior to, during, and after trial
        iii. Motion to dismiss for failure to state a claim, i.e., Demurrer. Under the lenient FRCP, it should seldom succeed. Can be raised during pleadings or trial. Rule 12(b)(6) addresses form. Only the pleadings are considered, not affidavits or any other evidence. FRCP 12(b)(6)
        iv. Clarification – complaint is too vague to respond to, request more details. FRCP 12(e)
        v. Failure to join a party needed for just adjudication (under FRCP 19) FRCP 12(b)(7)
        vi. Motion to Strike - allows P or D to have the court strike from the answer or reply any redundant, immaterial, impertinent, or scandalous matter that causes the other party prejudice. This motion is disfavored by the courts. FRCP 12(f)
        vii. Motion for a judgment on the pleadings. FRCP 12(c). A means for challenging the substantive sufficiency of the opposing party's pleadings *once all the pleadings have been completed*. Whereas the scope of a Rule 12(b)(6) motion is confined to the face of the complaint, a Rule 12(c) motion takes in all the pleadings on file. A motion for a judgment on the pleadings is converted into a FRCP 56 summary judgment motion if a party introduces extraneous materials in support of the motion. When such outside materials are allowed by the court, the opposing party must be given an opportunity to respond to the summary judgment motion.
    b. Answers
        viii. Deny
        ix. Affirmative Defense: must be presented *in the answer* or it is waived and cannot be introduced at trial. FRCP 8(c).
        x. Counterclaims(v. P), Cross-Claims(v. another D), and Third-Party claims (v. a new party)
g. Pleading Special Matters; FRCP 9(b)

6

i. In all averments of fraud or mistake, the circumstances constituting fraud or mistake shall be stated with *particularity*. Malice, intent, knowledge, and other conditions of mind of a person may be averred *generally*
ii. One can get the particulars by pleading on information and belief. FRCP 11(b)
iii. <u>Qualified Immunity</u> - government officials enjoy this privilege if they *reasonably* believe their actions were constitutional; therefore, the issue of state of mind is relevant in substantive law. Even though FRCP 9(b) states that conditions of the mind may be averred generally, with respect to cases challenging qualified immunity of government officials, the courts prefer that P alleges his complaint with particularity

h. Defendant Responses: Denials. FRCP 8(b)
   i. D can make "specific denials" of designated portions of the complaint
   ii. D can make "qualified general denial" that denies everything not expressly admitted
   iii. "General denials" of the whole complaint are usually improper. P will normally use FRCP 11 to combat this. Risk in using general denials: If D's denial does not *fairly meet the substance of the averments denied*, the court may deem D to have *admitted* P's specific averments. FRCP 8(b)
   iv. D can make a qualified denial
   v. D can deny based upon information and belief, which is a good faith belief that complaint is false but with insufficient first-hand knowledge by defendant to back it up
   vi. D can deny based on stating the he is without knowledge or information sufficient to form a belief

i. Plaintiff Reply (usually to a counterclaim by D)
   i. Normally P neither must nor may reply to an answer containing only defenses. FRCP 8(d)
   ii. FRCP 8(d) provides that the answer's averments are automatically taken to be "denied or avoided"
   iii. Very rarely the court may order a reply under FRCP 7(a) in the interests of clarification

j. Amendments to the Pleadings: FRCP 15
   a. Liberal amendment philosophy – apply to all pleadings: P's complaint, D's answer, P's reply (if filed), as well as pleadings relating to cross-claims and third-party claims
   b. Requests to amend pleadings may occur at three different times during the process of litigation
      1. Before a responsive pleading is served. A party may amend its pleading without the other party's or court's permission *at any time before a responsive pleading is served.* 15(a)
      2. When no responsive pleading permitted, pleader may amend the pleading at any time within 20 days after it is served, provided that the case has not already been placed on the court's calendar

3. Amendment at all other times by:
   a. Court's permission
   b. Written consent of the adverse parties
4. Leave to amend "freely given" unless:
   a. Undue delay
   b. Bad faith
   c. Dilatory motive
   d. Repeated failure to cure deficiencies by previous amendments
   e. Undue *prejudice* to the opposing party – being put at an unfair disadvantage. The burden is on the party objecting to the amendment to show prejudice or surprise if the leave to amend is granted. Even if there is prejudice to the defendant, the court can grant a continuance so defendant can cure its prejudice
   f. Futility of the amendment
c. Amendments to conform the pleadings: FRCP 15(b)
   i. Any party, at any time (even after trial) may assert a motion to conform the pleadings to the proof, even after a judgment
d. Failure to plead the issues: express and implied consent
   i. A party who has not raised issues in its pleadings but subsequentially introduces evidence in support of those issues at trial may do so through the implied consent of the opposing party. Consent will be implied if *the opposing party does not object to the introduction of evidence* in support of unpleaded issues
e. Standards for amendment at trial
   i. Prejudice to objecting party – the burden is on D to convince the court of the unfairness of permitting trial amendments of the pleadings to conform to the proof
   ii. Continuance – may be granted to the objecting party if amendment of the pleadings during trial is allowed. Gives the opposing party the opportunity to investigate and respond to the amended issues
f. Permissive amendments and statute of limitations: The relation-back doctrine. FRCP 15(c)
   i. In certain special circumstances, a party may be permitted to amend a pleading after a statute of limitations has run, and then the amended pleading "relates back" to the date of the original pleading. The relation-back doctrine then is a saving doctrine

that permits otherwise expired claims to be asserted, or mistaken parties to be changed or added to the litigation
ii. Circumstances permitting relation-back amendments
1. Where permitted by law – if the statute supplying the limitations permits the relation-back of an amendment. FRCP 15(c)(1)
2. The claim or defense asserted in the amended pleading arose out of the conduct, transaction, or occurrence set forth or attempted to be set forth in the original pleading. FRCP 15(c)(2)
   i. Some courts are less likely to permit amendments that add substantially different facts to the original allegations or change the focus of litigation
   ii. Same conduct, transaction, or occurrence is not a sharply defined concept
   iii. A defense lawyer should not stress that the amended claim is totally different, but rather, that it would cause prejudice
3. The amendment changes the party or the naming of the party against whom a claim is asserted if the foregoing provision 15(c)(2) is satisfied and, within the period provided by FRCP 4(m) for service of the summons and complaint (120 days), the party to be brought in by amendment (A) has received such notice of the institution of the action that the party will not be prejudiced in maintaining a defense on the merits, and (B) knew or should have known that, but for a mistake concerning the identity of the proper party, the action would have been brought against the party

III. DISCOVERY
a. Purposes of Discovery
   i. Preservation of evidence
   ii. Ascertainment of issues in controversy: pleadings contain many facts that are not in dispute. If the pleadings have put a claim in issue, it is legitimate to ask whether the pleader contests the facts underlying that issue

1. Admission of facts – via the "request for admissions". Requires the pleader to admit or deny factual allegations in the pleadings. Any factual matter admitted is not subject to subsequent proof or dispute. Matters that are not admitted may be disputed and must be proven at trial. FRCP 36
2. Prelude to summary judgment – discovery serves as a basis for a summary judgment motion
   iii. Evidence on issues in dispute: prelude to trial. Discovery is also used to ascertain relevant evidence to disputed factual issues that will be contested at trial
   1. Necessity for pretrial formal discovery devices – the discovery process provides a coercive means to obtain information from people who might not otherwise cooperate in supplying needed information
b. Scope and Discretionary Limits on Discovery
   i. Scope of Discovery
      1. General problem. The purpose of discovery is to permit the litigants to discover as much factual information as possible about both their own claims as well as the opposing party's defenses
      2. Procedure.
         a. Request. FRCP 27-36, 45(subpoena for non-parties)
         b. Objection. FRCP 26(b)(5), 30(d), 26(c)
         c. Conference. FRCP 37(a)(2)(b), 26(c)(protective order), 26(f)
         d. Court Order. FRCP 37(a)
         e. Sanctions. FRCP 37(b), 26(g)(like FRCP 11)
         f. Exceptions. FRCP 37(c), (d) allow immediate sanctions
      3. Standard. The standard for discovery under FRCP 26(b)(1) has five parts:
         a. "Any matter" – Discovery extends both to information relating to one's own case and information relating to the opposing party's case
         b. "Relevant to the subject matter involved in the action" – Courts interpret relevance broadly
         c. "Whether admissible (or not) at trial"
            i. Lawyers may obtain discovery of information that might not be admissible at trial. At deposition, a lawyer may ask questions that might be objectionable if asked at trial
            ii. Ex: Hearsay statements can be obtained even though they are not admissible at trial if they help the lawyer in ascertaining other information obtain the case
            iii. Insurance coverage. Parties are required to furnish, without a discovery request, copies of any insurance

agreements that exist to satisfy all or part of a judgment. FRCP 23(a)(1)(D)
            d. ***"Reasonably calculated to lead to the discovery of admissible evidence" FRCP 26(b)(1)
                i. Discovery must be justified, in some way, as assisting the litigant in finding information that will be admissible at trial
                ii. Ex: Information about trial tactics. Lawyers cannot probe into the trial strategy or tactics of the opposing party
                iii. Ex: D's assets. Lawyers cannot obtain general discovery of D's assets if the party's finances are not in issue
                iv. "Not privileged". Information cannot be covered by a privilege or immunity
            e. Information sought must not be unduly burdensome. FRCP 26(b)(2)
    c. Timing and Sequence of Discovery
        1. Initial discovery scheduling and conferences: FRCP 26(d),(f) and 16(b)
            a. General Prohibition. Parties generally may not seek discovery from any source before they have met and conferred as required by FRCP 26(f)
            b. Discovery meeting and agreement. Attorneys of record and all unrepresented parties must meet at least 14 days prior to scheduling conference with a federal district judge. FRCP 26(f). At this meeting, the parties must, in good faith, discuss their claims and defenses and possible settlement, arrange for informal exchange of the information required under FRCP 26(a)(1), and develop a proposed formal discovery plan
            c. Court-mandated scheduling order: FRCP 16(b). When the federal court receives the parties' FRCP 26(f) written report, the court will confer with the attorneys by phone, mail, or person and issue a scheduling order
        2. Mandatory informal exchange of information: FRCP 26(a)(1)
            a. Required disclosures. Without awaiting a discovery request parties must now disclose the names, addresses, and telephone numbers of individuals likely to have discoverable information relevant to disputed facts *alleged with particularity* in the pleadings, identifying the subjects of the information; descriptions and locations of documents, data compilations, and tangible things in the possession, custody or control of a party that are relevant to the disputed facts *alleged with particularity in the pleadings*; a computation of damages the disclosing party

claims, as well as documents or other evidence supporting the calculation of those damages (and including materials bearing on the nature and extent of injuries); and any insurance agreement which may satisfy or indemnify all or part of a judgment
    b. Timing of informal information exchange. Parties are required to exchange FRCP 26(a)(1) information at or within 10 days after they meet to discuss the litigation required in FRCP 26(f) (See 3(1)(a) Supra). FRCP 26(f) requires the attorneys meet at least 14 days before the FRCP 16 scheduling conference, and to submit a written report no later than 10 days after their meeting. FRCP 16 scheduling conference, at the latest, will occur either 90 or 120 days after the defendant makes an appearance or the plaintiff serves the complaint
    c. Expert Witnesses: The 1993 amended discovery rules require parties to disclose the identity of any expert witness to be used at trial
        i. Expert witness report and opinions. Parties must supply expert witness reports of retained, *testifying* expert witnesses. The report must state the expert's qualifications, publications, and other cases in which the expert has testified within four years. FRCP 26(a)(2)
        ii. After disclosure, testifying experts may be deposed. FRCP 26(b)(4)(a)
        iii. Non-Testifying experts. FRCP 26(a)(2) does not require disclosure of the identity or opinions of non-testifying experts, and FRCP 26(b)(4)(b) provides that a party may only seek discovery concerning non-testifying experts upon a showing of "exceptional" circumstances
    d. Pretrial disclosures: FRCP 26(a)(3). Prior to trial, in addition to early disclosure and expert witness information, parties also must disclose certain evidentiary material that will be used for other than impeachment purposes
d. Discretionary Limits on Scope of Discovery in Adversary System
   1. There are three primary ways of protecting information from disclosure during discovery: through invocation of a valid privilege, immunity, or protective order
      1. Privileges in general. FRCP 26(b)(1) permits discovery of matter that is "not privileged". In general, the same rules of privilege that apply at trial also apply during discovery, and the "reasonably calculated to lead to discovery of admissible evidence" standard of FRCP 26(b)(1) does not circumvent privilege

- a. Privileges at common law. The common law has long recognized various testimonial privileges, including communications between attorney and client, doctor and patient, priest and penitent, and husband and wife. State law determines the existence and scope of these privileges. Some states have limited spousal immunity. In addition, almost no jurisdiction recognizes a privilege for reporter and source
- b. Testimonial privileges. Testimonial privileges include the privilege against self-incrimination, testifying against a spouse, and revealing the identity of confidential police informants

2. Attorney-client privilege
    - a. Attorney-client privilege in federal court: Source of authority. In purely federal claims, attorney-client privilege is a matter of federal law. In federal diversity cases, attorney-client privilege is governed by state common law principles. See Federal Rule of Evidence 501
    - b. ***Scope. If the attorney-client privilege is validly invoked, it attaches to all communications between the client and the client's attorney. Elements:
        - i. Confidential Information
        - ii. Between Client
        - iii. And *Attorney*
        - iv. For the purpose of seeking legal advice
    - c. How invoked; burdens of proof. The person claiming the attorney-client privilege must invoke it in response to a discovery request, and carries the burden of establishing the existence of the privilege. Parties must expressly claim the privilege in response to a discovery request. FRCP 26(b)(5)
    - d. Possessor of the privilege. The client possesses the privilege and must invoke it. As a practical matter, the attorney invokes the privilege on the client's behalf
    - e. Nature of the privilege. Attorney-client privilege is *absolute*. If the privilege exists, it bars disclosure of the protected information. It is not a qualified privilege, and cannot be overcome on a showing of need for the information by the party requesting disclosure (cp. Work Product doctrine, which is a *qualified immunity*).
    - f. Qualifications, waivers, and exceptions. Attorney-client privilege is subject to certain qualifications, exceptions, and waivers. The following information is not protected by attorney-client privilege: facts, disclosures by consent or waiver, involuntary or inadvertent disclosures, independent information obtained by either attorney or client, ongoing or future crimes, frauds, or torts

3. Attorney Work Product doctrine
    a. Work product immunity is primarily a protection of the lawyer, rather than the client
    b. Attorney work product doctrine in federal court: Sources of authority. The two major authoritative sources of work product doctrine in federal court are the Supreme Court's 1947 decision in *Hickman v. Taylor* and the 1970 codification of the doctrine in FRCP 26(b)(3)
    c. FRCP 26(b)(3) permits discovery of *ordinary* work product:
        i. Documents and tangible things. Anything related to the party's position is discoverable: depositions and witness statements
        ii. By attorney, client, or agents of party
        iii. *** Any memoranda, notes, or working papers created by an attorney in *anticipation of litigation* is protected from disclosure by the work-product doctrine
    d. *Opinion* work product consists of an attorney's "mental impressions, conclusions, opinions, notes, or legal theories prepared in anticipation of litigation." Opinion work product is protected from disclosure and may not be compelled, even upon a showing of substantial need. A minority of federal courts engage in a balancing test to determine whether an opinion work product may be ordered to be disclosed. See *Xerox Corp. v. International Business Machs. Corp.* (ordering production of lawyer's notes of interviews with defendant's employees who could not recall crucial information at depositions; parties cannot conceal information by imparting it to a lawyer and then hiding behind work product immunity). The protection extends to the opinion work product of other party representatives
    e. *Hickman* and FRCP 26(b)(3) compared. The federal work product rule is considered to be a partial codification of the Supreme Court's holding in *Hickman*. Ex: The federal rule covers only "documents and tangible things", but *Hickman* extends work product protection to intangible work product, such as oral statements. Federal courts typically refer to both the Supreme Court's holding in *Hickman* and FRCP 26(b)(3) as authoritative sources for the work product doctrine
    f. How invoked; burdens of proof. The person claiming attorney work product immunity must invoke it in response to a discovery request, and carries the burden of establishing the existence of the immunity. FRCP 26(b)(5):

Parties must expressly claim the immunity in response to a discovery request
- g. Overcoming the immunity. Once the party invoking the immunity states the grounds for the immunity's existence, the party seeking disclosure carries the burden of overcoming the immunity by showing *substantial need* for the requested materials and an inability to obtain a substantial equivalent by other means (undue hardship)
- h. Qualifications, waivers, and exceptions. Attorney work product immunity is subject to the same qualifications, waivers, and exceptions as attorney-client privilege. See C.4(2)(f) supra. In addition to this list of exceptions, work product immunity also excludes "party statements" from work product protection. Information obtained by interrogatories is not protected by work product **Hickman**. FRCP 33(c)

4. Protective Orders: FRCP 26(c)
    - a. Although the FRCP enable liberal discovery, the manner and scope of discovery may be tailored to protect against embarrassment, harassment, or release of certain proprietary information (such as trade secrets). Parties may shield such information through a "protective order"
    - b. Stipulated agreements. Parties may negotiate protective orders or confidentiality agreements, and may stipulate to the terms of such agreements. If the parties cannot agree, then a person seeking to shield information may file a motion for a protective order
    - c. Umbrella protective orders. Lawyers in complex litigation sometimes agree to an "umbrella" protective order at the outset of litigation that covers entire categories of materials. This arrangement avoids the necessity of having a court determine whether to issue a protective order on a document-by-document basis
    - d. Court-mandated protective orders: who may seek. The party seeking a protective order must furnish the court with a certificate that the lawyers have conferred in good faith and attempted to resolve the discovery dispute. FRCP 26(d)
    - e. Standards. In its discretion, a court may issue an order "which justice requires to protect a party or person from undue annoyance, embarrassment, oppression, or undue burden or expense." FRCP 26(d)
    - f. In camera inspection. When a party seeks a protective order relating to information contained in documents, courts examine the documents *in camera ex parte*, i.e., a judge reviews the materials in chambers w/o the presence of the party seeking discovery

g. Denial of protective orders: Expenses. If a court denies a motion for a protective order, the court may order discovery. The court also may award expenses incurred in relation to the motion. FRCP 37(a)(4)
h. First Amendment concerns. There is no first amendment right to obtain or disseminate information obtained through discovery. See ***Seattle Times Co. v. Rhinehart***

e. Physical and Mental Examinations: FRCP 35
  1. Constitutional privacy concerns. FRCP 35 is constitutional. The Supreme court has twice ruled that FCP 35 does not impermissibly violate the **Rules Enabling Act, 28 U.S.C. §§ 2017-2072** by creating substantive law
     a. State law has power over the FRCP
     b. Art. I, §8 and Art. III, §1 of the Constitution govern the Rules Enabling Act, which governs the FRCP
     c. 28 USC §2072 (b): FRCP shall not abridge, enlarge, or modify any substantive right
  2. Order for examination: standards
     a. When the mental or physical condition (including the blood group) of a party is in *controversy*, the court in which the action is pending may order the party to submit to a physical or mental examination by a suitably licensed or certified examiner. FRCP 35
        i. Person in party's custody or legal control. A court may order that a party "produce for examination the person in the party's custody or legal control." A party can only be required to make a *good faith effort* to produce the person to be examined. If a proposed examinee refuses to cooperate with the request, an examination can be avoided and *no sanctions are available.* FRCP 37(b)(2)(E)
     b. Condition in controversy. A person's physical or mental condition is in controversy if it is directly in issue in the litigation. A person's condition also may be in controversy if it has substantial bearing on facts in issue.
     c. Showing good cause. No party may obtain a court order for a physical or mental examination unless the party has shown good cause for the request. A defendant in a personal injury suit demonstrates good cause by showing that he has not had an opportunity to make an independent analysis of P's condition
        i. Information from other sources. If D is able to obtain information about P's condition from other sources, then good cause is not shown

f. Sanctions

1. Availability of discovery sanctions in general. Sanctions are available only when the discovery process breaks down and the aggrieved party seeks a court order requiring a person to attend a deposition, answer interrogatories, or produce requested documents. FRCP 37(a)
2. Before a court will give an order compelling an answer to the discovery request, the movant must have conferred or attempted to confer with the opposing party in order to resolve the matter without court action. FRCP 37(a)(2)(b)
3. Contempt. Contempt sanctions usually cannot be issued for failure to comply with discovery requests, b/c the initial discovery request typically is not made under compulsion of a court order
4. Jurisdictional issues. Only a court with personal jurisdiction over a witness may issue an order compelling the witness to make discovery requests. FRCP 37(a)(1)
5. Signature requirements
    a. Signature requirements for early mandatory exchange of information: FRCP 26(g)(1)
    b. Signature requirements for discovery requests and responses: FRCP 26(g)(2). B/C most violations of the discovery rules can also be construed as violations of the signature requirements, Rule 26(g) may encourage federal courts to impose discovery sanctions more often *without an intervening order compelling discovery*. The attorney's signature constitutes the lawyer's certification that to the best of the signer's knowledge, information, and belief, formed after a reasonable inquiry, that a request, response, or objection is:
        i. Consistent with the discovery rules and warranted by existing law or a good faith argument *for the extension, modification, or reversal of existing law*
        ii. Not interposed for any improper purpose, such as to harass or cause unnecessary delay or needless increase in the cost of litigation
        iii. Not unreasonable or unduly burdensome or expensive, given the needs of the case, the discovery already had in the case, the amount in controversy, and the importance of the issues at stake in the litigation
        iv. Over-discovery. Rule 26(g) also supplies the sole authority under the rules for imposing sanctions for *over-discovery*
6. Court-ordered discovery: possible sanctions
    a. Even where discovery is court-ordered, federal courts have been reluctant to sanction non-complying parties, and generally will do so only if there is willful non-compliance.

However, when a party fails to comply, courts have an array of possible sanctions. FRCP 37(b), (c), (d)
- b. Contempt. Once a court has issued a discovery order, a non-responding party may be held in contempt for failure to comply with the court order. A party held in contempt may be fined or jailed until such time as he or she complies with the discovery request. FRCP 37(b)(2)(d), (e)
    - i. Failure to submit to a physical or mental examination. A person may not be jailed for a refusal to submit to a physical or mental examination. Other less direct sanctions are available under FRCP 37(b)(2)(d), (e)
- c. Attorney's fees. A party that has been unreasonable in refusing to comply with a discovery request may be assessed the opposing counsel's attorney's fees incurred in seeking the motion. FRCP 37(a)(4); (b)(2)(e); (c)(2); (d)
- d. Striking portions of claims or defenses. A court may sanction a party who receives notice of a deposition and fails to appear, or fails to answer interrogatories, by striking all or a portion of a claim or defense. FRCP 37(b)(2)
- e. Other possible sanctions: default, dismissal, limiting trial testimony. FRCP 37(b)(2)

7. Summary of Authority for Sanction
    - a. FRCP 37
        - i. 37(a)(4). A party may seek an award for expenses, including attorney's fees, incurred in a connection with a motion to compel. "The loser pays"
        - ii. 37(b)(2)(e). Authorizes sanctions where a party fails to comply with court-ordered discovery
        - iii. 37(c). Provides a self-executing sanction for a party's prejudicial failure to disclose information required to be disclosed by FRCP 26(a), by precluding that party from using the information as evidence at trial
        - iv. 37(d). When the discoveree simply refuses to respond, i.e., fails to appear at all for his deposition, or to serve any response to interrogatories or production requests, then *the predicate of a discovery order is eliminated*, and the discoverer can move directly for sanctions short of contempt and for all expenses caused by the failure of discovery, not just those incurred in making the Rule 37(d) motion
        - v. 37(g). Provides for the award of expenses against an attorney who fails to participate in good faith in the framing of a discovery plan under FRCP 26(f)

b. 28 U.S.C. § 1927
    i. Sanctions may be imposed against any attorney "who so multiplies the proceedings in any case to increase the costs unreasonably and vexatiously". An attorney who engages in such conduct may be personally liable for excess costs, expenses, and attorney's fees. Imposition of sanctions under § 1927 requires a clear showing of bad faith: "an award is proper when the attorney's actions are so completely without merit as to require the conclusion that they must have been taken for some improper purpose such as delay".
c. Inherent Power
    i. Courts have the power "to manage their own affairs so as to achieve the orderly and expeditious disposition of cases" **Chambers v. NASCO**. This power embraces the authority to impose costs and attorneys' fees against a party or his attorney where a party has acted in bad faith, vexatiously, wantonly, or for oppressive reasons
d. FRCP 30
    i. Any objection during a deposition is to be stated concisely and in a non-argumentative and non-suggestive manner. FRCP 30(d)(1)
    ii. Sanctions, including costs and attorneys' fees, may be awarded under Rule 30 for conduct which a court finds has frustrated the fair examination of the deponent. FRCP 30(d)(2)

IV. RESOLUTION WITHOUT TRIAL

a. FRCP 55: Default Judgment
    i. A party is in default and subject to the rules governing default judgments when he "fails to *plead* or otherwise defend" as by filing motions to attack the adversary's pleadings
b. FRCP 41(a): Voluntary Dismissal or Nonsuit
    i. P can obtain dismissal of his suit without prejudice to his opportunity to litigate the same claim later
    ii. P may dismiss without leave of court by filing notice of dismissal before an answer or motion for summary judgment is served upon him
    iii. After an issue is joined by the service of an answer or motion for summary judgment, P may voluntarily dismiss only by stipulation of the parties or by order of the court upon such terms and conditions as it deems proper
c. FRCP 41(b): Involuntary Dismissal or Compulsory Nonsuit
    i. Disobedience that would justify dismissal also often consists of litigation delays, or of failures to appear, respond or take other required action.

Because these matters threaten the trial court's control over its docket, it follows that it may draw on its inherent powers to dismiss P's action *sua sponte*

ii. Involuntary dismissals and compulsory nonsuits are with prejudice to reinstitution of the action, unless otherwise provided or unless grounded on failure of a precondition to suit. Jurisdiction, proper venue, or joinder of a party under FRCP 19 are such preconditions. Dismissals based on P's failure to satisfy these conditions do not operate as adjudications upon the merits

d. Summary of Default
   i. FRCP 12(a) time limit
   ii. FRCP 55(a) default
   iii. FRCP 55(b) default judgment
   iv. FRCP 54(c) amount of judgment
   v. FRCP 55(c) set aside default
   vi. FRCP 60(b) set aside judgment

e. Due Process
   i. State Action
   ii. Deprivation of liberty or property
   iii. Improper procedure
   iv. W/o notice and opportunity to be heard

f. FRCP 56: Summary Judgment
   i. The summary judgment motion permits a party to go *beyond the pleadings* to show that there is no genuine dispute of material fact that would necessitate or justify the expense of trial, and to argue that the court should enter judgment for him on some or all claims and defenses as a matter of law
   ii. The moving party may satisfy FRCP 56's burden of production in two ways:
      1. Submit affirmative evidence that *negates* an essential element of the nonmoving party's claim
      2. Demonstrate to the court that the nonmoving party's evidence is *insufficient* to establish an essential element of the nonmoving party's claim
   iii. Does evidence + reasonable inferences + substantive law lead to plaintiff's recovery ?
      1. Yes – Continue with the case
      2. No – Throw out the case, rule for defendant
   iv. When admissible material is offered in support of a FRCP 12(b)(6) motion to dismiss for failure to state a claim or a FRCP 12(c) motion for judgment on the pleadings, these federal rules provide that the motions shall be treated as summary judgment motions
   v. When evidentiary material in the record suggests the availability of summary judgment, a federal court may grant summary judgment *sua sponte*

      vi. Partial Summary Judgment. Allows the court to dispose of certain issues while saving others for trial. FRCP 56(d). Thus, the partial summery judgment says no material issue of fact exists to those issues for which the motion is granted, but preserves the rest for trial
      vii. Time limits. A plaintiff has 20 days to make a summary judgment motion after the action is commenced. FRCP 56(a). A defendant may make a summary judgment motion at any time. FRCP 56(b)
      viii. Responses to the Motion. Plaintiff may give any of three responses:
1. Present an *affidavit* under FRCP 56(f) stating why he cannot now present facts in opposition to summary judgment. Since summary judgment motions can be filed at any time, this rule allows the plaintiff time to undertake discovery
2. Do nothing. The burden of production is on the movant to make a *prima facie* showing that there is no genuine dispute of material fact. To avoid summary judgment the opposing party may not rest upon the mere allegations or denials of his pleading, but his response by *affidavits* or otherwise as provided in the rule, must set forth *specific facts* showing that there is a genuine issue for trial. FRCP 56(e)
3. Affidavits shall be made on:
   a. Personal knowledge, not opinion or hearsay
   b. Shall set forth such facts as would be admissible in evidence
   c. Shall show affirmatively that the affiant is competent to testify to the matters stated therein
4. Cross-motion for summary judgment. The plaintiff does not concede the absence of genuine issues on the initial motion by filing the cross-motion
      ix. The Supreme Court has declared that the standard for summary judgment mirrors the standard for judgment as a matter of law (FRCP 50): "the trial judge must direct a verdict, if under the governing law, there can be but one reasonable conclusion as to the verdict" Therefore, the judge must determine whether a reasonable jury could resolve the issue for the non-movant by a preponderance of the evidence

g. Settlement
    i. Usually done during pretrial conference. FRCP 16(a)(5)
    ii. When defendant's highest offer overlaps with plaintiff's lowest acceptable offer there will be settlement
    iii. Arbitration is a cheaper way to achieve adjudication, but it decreases the settlement range
    iv. Settlement reservation price:
1. Plaintiff = Probability of Judgment (Value of Judgment) – relative cost of total trial
2. Defendant = Probability of Judgment (Value of Judgment) + relative cost of total trial

V. TRIAL

a. Right to Trial by Jury. FRCP 38, 7th Amendment to Constitution
   i. Upon timely written demand of any party, there will be trial by jury on those contested factual issues:
   ii. That are triable of right by a jury under the *Seventh Amendment* to the Federal Constitution, which is read expansively and includes at least any issue arising in a case such that the issue would have been triable of right to a common-law jury in 1791, i.e., the issue was *not* tried in a court of equity in 1791
   iii. Equity
      1. Relief is injunctions
      2. Fact finder is judge
   iv. Law
      1. Relief is damages
      2. Fact finder is jury
   v. That are triable of right by a jury under some federal *statute*
   vi. Also, the court, in its discretion with the *consent* of both parties, can order a trial by jury under FRCP 39(c)
   vii. State jury practice is widely similar to federal. However, the Seventh Amendment and its expansive reading do *not* apply to the states
   viii. Claiming a jury trial. FRCP 38(b): Any party may demand a trial by jury of any issue triable of right by jury by serving upon the other parties a demand therefore in writing at any time after the commencement of the action and not later than 10 days after the service of the last pleading directed to such issue
b. Controlling the Jury
   i. Jurors use the evidence to answer factual questions
   ii. But, only the judge can resolve issues about the meaning or application of law
   iii. One way in which the judge must maintain legal control is in the way he instructs (charges) the jury
   iv. FRCP 51. Instructions to Jury
      1. At the close of the evidence any party may file written requests that the court instruct the jury on the law as set forth in the requests
      2. A party may challenge instructions on appeal only if he earlier objects before the jury retires to consider its verdict, stating distinctly the matter objected to and the grounds of the objection
      3. Jury instructions have two audiences, the jury and the appellate court
   v. FRCP 49. Verdicts
      1. In the usual civil jury trial, the jury is charged with returning a *general verdict*, i.e., a verdict for one side or another supplying no explanation why the jury decided as it did
         a. Such verdicts are in extensive use and work well in simple cases
         b. The weakness is that they fail to illuminate the jury's decision making process

- c. It is easy for the jury to ignore constraints and admonitions in the charge when it can hide behind the general verdict
- d. It is also difficult to preserve the work of the jury if problems arise with the case on appeal of a general verdict
2. The *special verdict* is an alternative intended to address these shortcomings
    - a. Jury instructions designed to elicit a special verdict contain a series of short-answer fact questions
    - b. The jurors answer the questions instead of designating a winner
    - c. From all the answers, the judge constructs the equivalent of a general verdict
    - d. If the answers appear inconsistent, the judge is obliged to attempt to reconcile the jury's findings, by exegesis if necessary before either resubmitting them or ordering a new trial
    - e. Parties don't have a right to a special verdict, they can only request one
    - f. FRCP 49(b). A comprise to the special verdict; a general verdict accompanied with answers to written interrogatories
        - i. This verdict form permits jurors to declare a winner, but requires them to show their work
        - ii. However, it is even more vulnerable to inconsistencies than the special verdict, since the jury's answers may be inconsistent not only with each other, but also with the general verdict
- vi. Harmless Error. FRCP 61
    1. The court at every stage of the proceeding must disregard any error or defect in the proceeding which does not affect the substantial rights of the parties
- c. Directed verdicts and Judgment notwithstanding the verdict. FRCP 50
    - i. Directed verdict. After trial has begun, a party may by motion request the court to render judgment without letting the case go to a jury verdict
    - ii. Judgment notwithstanding the verdict (j.n.o.v.). If a verdict has been entered, the losing party may request the judge to render a decision opposed to that indicated by the verdict. FRCP 50(a). The party must have requested a directed verdict during the trial in order to request a jnov. FRCP 50(b)
    - iii. The ground for both motions is that the evidence presented would support only one result. There is no legally sufficient evidentiary basis for a *reasonable jury* to find for the party on the issue contested. FRCP 50 and FRCP 56 have the same standards
    - iv. How to decide to grant these motions? *Substantial evidence test*. Evidence is substantial when it is capable of providing a *reasonable* basis for a juror to find for the party opposing the directed verdict or jnov

- v. Producing just some evidence cannot satisfy the burden of production; the moving party must submit evidence so that a reasonable inference can be drawn. See **Celotex**
- d. New Trial Motions. FRCP 59
  - i. The most widely used form of judicial control of juries is the order granting a new trial on all or some part of the issues
  - ii. The availability of a new trial is restricted to ten days after the verdict is returned or judgment is entered
  - iii. FRCP 59(a) authorizes new trials for a multitude of reasons. Most grounds for a new trial fall into two categories:
    1. Errors in the jury's evaluation of the evidence
       a. When the trial judge concludes that the verdict is excessive, inadequate, or otherwise *against the weight of the evidence*, he is second-guessing the jury in its evaluation of the evidence
       b. Unlike directed verdict or jnov, an order for a new trial does not deprive the verdict-winner of jury trial; it only forces him to submit his evidence to a new jury
       c. The judge can grant the motion for a new trial, and usually will do so unless the opposing party agrees to a reduction (*remittitur*) of the verdict. The party who consents to remittitur waives any right to appellate review of it
    2. Errors in the trial process, including errors in the law applied (abuse of discretion). Errors include:
       a. Judicial errors in instructing the jury
       b. Judicial errors in admitting or commenting on the evidence
       c. Misconduct by parties, counsel, witnesses, or jurors
       d. Prejudicial happenstance
- e. Nonjury Trials. FRCP 52
  - i. The court does not have as much discretion in findings of fact as a jury since 7th amendment concerns are not present
  - ii. Findings of fact, whether based on oral or documentary evidence, shall not be set aside unless *clearly erroneous*, and due regard shall be given to the opportunity of the trial court to judge of the credibility of witnesses. FRCP 52(a)
  - iii. When an error does arise in a bench trial, the court often simply rehears part of the case or reconsiders its decision

VI. PERSONAL JURISDICTION AND VENUE
  a. Law which limits the reach of *state* courts' territorial jurisdiction
  - i. The primary restraint on the territorial jurisdiction of state courts is the Due Process Clause of the 14th Amendment to the United States Constitution. The clause provides that "no State shall deprive any person of life, liberty, or *property*, without due process of law"
  - ii. A cause of action is "property" within the meaning of the Clause, which cannot be forfeited through state proceedings lacking due process

iii. The protections of due process are similarly available to those against whom claims are made
iv. The Due Process Clause also affords litigants rights to notice and the opportunity to be heard in state court
v. Most state courts enjoy only as much territorial jurisdiction over nonresident defendants as their legislatures have chosen to confer by statute. All states now have long-arm statutes which endow their courts with all or nearly all the jurisdictional authority permitted by due process

b. Law which limits the reach of *federal* courts' territorial jurisdiction
   i. The 14th Amendment does not apply to federal courts. However, the authority of federal courts is limited by the same Due Process Clause appearing in the 5th Amendment to the Constitution
   ii. Yet, the Constitution does not limit federal courts to the same degree. It is at least arguable that the 5th Amendment permits federal courts to exercise territorial jurisdiction over all United States citizens
   iii. However, Congress has created, via statutes, nationwide territorial jurisdiction for federal courts in only a few special circumstances. FRCP 4(k)(1)(D) Ex: Statutes involving securities
   iv. ***Absent such a statute, federal courts will be limited to the jurisdictional reach of a local state court. This limitation results from FRCP 4(k)(1)(A)'s provision that service or waiver of service will establish jurisdiction over any defendant "who could be subjected to the jurisdiction of a court of general jurisdiction in the state in which the district court is located"
   v. By this indirect route federal judges usually find themselves laboring under the same 14th Amendment due process and state law limitations as their state court counterparts
   vi. This means that federal courts often do not direct their concerns over territorial jurisdiction to a body of distinctly federal law
   vii. This is in marked contrast to the preeminent role federal law plays in resolving questions of federal subject matter jurisdiction
   viii. The 1993 amendment to Rule 4 authorizes nationwide service of process to establish personal jurisdiction over any defendant who is not subject to the jurisdiction of the courts of jurisdiction of any state. FRCP 4(k)(2). This mainly applies to aliens. Aliens would be subject to the new subsection only when minimum contacts existed between them and the United States *but* did not exist between them and any state

c. PERSONAL JURISDICTION OVERVIEW
   i. Power
      1. Due Process. **International Shoe**
      2. Long Arm
      3. FRCP 4(k) – Federal Courts
   ii. Notice
      1. Due Process. **Mullane**
      2. Service. FRCP 4(d) – (j)

d. *In Personam* Jurisdiction

i. Also called Personal Jurisdiction. Provides courts with a basis for entirely determining controversies involving personal obligations (often tort or contract claims)
ii. Because the court's jurisdiction is over the person of the defendant, it can impose judgment indebtedness upon him to the *full extent of the wrong* done to the plaintiff
iii. If an *in personam* judgment for damages cannot be fully satisfied where rendered, plaintiff may collect the unsatisfied portion of the judgment in any other state or federal court. "The Full Faith and Credit Clause makes the valid *in personam* judgment of one State enforceable in all other States" **Shaffer v. Heitner**

e. *In Rem* Jurisdiction
   i. *In rem* jurisdiction focuses not on the person of the defendant but on some property located within the forum
   ii. Courts use this form of jurisdiction to adjudicate questions concerning the ownership and control of such property

f. *Quasi In Rem* Jurisdiction
   i. Like *in rem* jurisdiction, *quasi in rem* jurisdiction operates on property located within the forum and not directly against the person of individual defendants
   ii. *Also like in rem* judgment, a *quasi in rem* judgment binds the parties *only with reference to their interests in the res upon which jurisdiction is based* (the value of a *quasi in rem* judgment cannot exceed the value of the *res*) Therefore, *in rem* and *quasi in rem* judgments usually have no effect elsewhere
   iii. But like *in personam* jurisdiction, *quasi in rem* jurisdiction is used to adjudicate personal obligations

g. Traditionally Accepted forms of Personal Jurisdiction
   i. Suits in the defendant's home state
      1. Courts of the defendant's home state traditionally have personal jurisdiction over the defendant
      2. Which state is home for the defendant?
         a. For defendants who are natural persons, *domicile* might seem to provide the best standard
         b. A legally competent person acquires a domicile by being present there with the intention of making the place his home. Every person has a domicile, but never more than one
         c. *In personam* jurisdiction may be deemed improper in the state of a person's domicile if the party has left his domicile and not yet established a new one. Residence is a better concept to use here
   ii. Personal jurisdiction over *nonresidents* through *waiver* or express consent
      1. Because the requirement of personal jurisdiction represents an individual right, it can, like other such rights, be waived

2. Waiver need not be express. It is enough that a party act in a way which is incompatible with his argument that the forum lacks a basis for asserting personal jurisdiction over him
    a. Ex: A nonresident *plaintiff* waives due process objections to the court's jurisdiction by filing suit in the forum. This is, by availing himself of the forum's judicial process, he must now defend against cross-claims and counterclaims in the forum
3. Since it is unlikely that a court will respond to a defect in personal jurisdiction on its own initiative, a nonresident *defendant* must move for dismissal. Procedural systems provide mechanisms for the defendant to appear and question the court's personal jurisdiction without curing plaintiff's problem in the process
4. The defendant will not prejudice his motion to dismiss by joining with it other grounds for dismissal
5. However care must be taken even in courts that follow the federal model. Defendant will *waive* his challenge to personal jurisdiction if he either fails to include it in a motion to dismiss made on other grounds, *or fails to raise the matter by motion or pleading*. FRCP 12(h)(1)
6. Denial of a motion to dismiss for lack of personal jurisdiction is an interlocutory order (cannot be appealed). One must argue on the merits, then appeal. Federal courts permit the defendant to renew his objection to the court's personal jurisdiction, even though he has fully contested the case during the interim
7. Defendant may also lose, i.e, *waive*, his personal jurisdiction challenge as a penalty under FRCP 37(b)(2)(a) for failure to comply with an order compelling discovery. **Insurance Corp. of Ireland v. Compagnie des Bauxites**

iii. Jurisdiction by Consent
1. Forum-Selection Clauses in contracts both consent to jurisdiction in a particular court and bar litigation in any other court. Some courts refused to enforce the second, anti-jurisdiction feature of the clause. However, in **Carnival Cruise Lines v. Shute**, the Supreme court upheld such a clause that had appeared on the back of an injured plaintiff's steamship ticket
2. Forum selection clauses are invalid if:
    a. They were not freely bargained for
    b. Create additional expense for one party
    c. Deny one party a remedy
3. There are two aspects of consent to consider:
    a. Procedural – Was consent achieved in a manner the customers could understand? Ex: Was the type large enough? Was there adequate notice?
    b. Substantive – Was the contract fair? Ex: Florida was the home of Carnival's operations, so it is fair to have Florida as the forum, as opposed to, say, London

- iv. Transient Jurisdiction
    1. Transient Jurisdiction is based on service within the forum of a nonresident defendant who happens to be passing through the state
- h. Timing the Jurisdictional Challenge
    - i. Direct Attack
        1. Defendant participates in the lawsuit. Defendant joins with his jurisdictional attack other reasons why plaintiff's suit should be dismissed and he also resists the merits as well
        2. Problem with direct attack is that it forces the defendant to give up part of the protection secured by due process by forcing him to participate in the lawsuit, and sometimes, to defend on the merits
    - ii. Collateral Attack
        1. A defendant is always free to ignore the judicial proceedings, risk a default judgment, and then challenge that judgment on jurisdictional grounds in a collateral proceeding.
        2. Courts will usually entertain collateral attack for lack of personal jurisdiction *only* if the defendant took no part whatsoever in the initial proceeding. By claiming a lack of personal jurisdiction and then not arguing the case on the merits, Insurance Corp. submitted itself to a "primordial" form of personal jurisdiction. **Insurance Corp. of Ireland v. Compagnie des Bauxites**
        3. There are two grounds on which a defendant can base a collateral attack:
            a. Lack of notice. Defendants may assert denial of the notice and opportunity to be heard guaranteed by due process
            b. Unenforceability of the judgment where rendered. A court need not enforce a foreign judgment if the rendering system would not enforce it
- i. **International Shoe v. Washington**. Beginning of the modern era
    - i. Plaintiff's power to require defendant to participate where plaintiff chooses is limited by the scope of personal jurisdiction permitted by due process
    - ii. Due process will limit plaintiff to "reasonable" choices and tells us that an important focus for determining jurisdiction will be on the "contacts" that corporate defendant has with the forum state
    - iii. *** For a nonresident defendant who cannot be found and served within the forum state, **International Shoe** announced that good personal jurisdiction requires that the defendant have certain *minimum contacts* with the forum, and that maintenance of the suit does not offend "traditional notions of fair play and substantial justice"
    - iv. Personal jurisdiction would not necessarily require service of process to be completed within the forum. Silent on whether service on the defendant would invariably create good personal jurisdiction
    - v. Location within the forum of facts about the controversy and the defendant is more important than whether service of process was completed there
    - vi. Types of "contacts" a nonresident defendant could have with the forum:
        1. Substantial business related to plaintiff's claim

- a. Ex: Defendant has a factory makes shoes in WA. Benefits are the protection accorded by the laws and government of WA. Burdens are showing up and defending the action in a state where one has a factory (minimal burden). Conclusion: personal jurisdiction established
2. Insubstantial business unrelated to plaintiff's claim
    - a. Ex: Plaintiff injured in CA, sues defendant in WA. Defendant's only contact with the forum is 10 salesmen in WA, no factory present. Benefits are minimal, no employees in WA. Burdens are high, no information available in WA. Conclusion: no personal jurisdiction
3. Substantial business unrelated to plaintiff's claim
    - a. Ex: Salesman traveling through WA, lands in WA airport. Benefits: some, can land in WA. Burdens: very high, in an action for unemployment taxes the defendant has no information. Conclusion: no personal jurisdiction
4. Insubstantial business related to plaintiff's claim (actual **Shoe** case)
    - a. Benefits are low, WA state creates a market for sales. Burdens are some, salesman have to travel a lot. Conclusion: personal jurisdiction established
- j. Modifications on personal jurisdiction as a result of International Shoe
    1. **Hanson v. Denckla**. The Court's isolated warning
        - a. The Delaware trust companies did not conduct "continuous and systematic" operations in the forum
        - b. They had no offices in Florida and transacted no business there
        - c. The controversy centered on the validity of the trust, and the trust was created in Delaware
        - d. Therefore, the trustees directed little if any of their activities at the forum state. The trustees did not have minimal contacts with Florida
        - e. *** The court discounted the significance of contacts between the plaintiffs and the forum, stating that "*unilateral activity* of those who claim some relationship with a nonresident defendant cannot satisfy the requirement of contact with the forum State"
        - f. *** Purposeful availment. The defendant must *purposefully* avail itself of the privilege of conducting activities within the forum State, thereby invoking the benefits and protections of its laws. That is, the defendant must have made a deliberate choice to relate to the state in some meaningful way, and *expected* some benefits from the forum state
    2. **Shaffer v. Heitner**. Minimum contacts and the decline of *quasi in rem* jurisdiction
        - a. Delaware may have lacked minimum contacts necessary to support personal jurisdiction over the defendants since they

            did not reside there and the alleged wrongful acts occurred outside Delaware
        b. Plaintiff attempted to avoid the problem by proceeding upon a *quasi in rem* theory of jurisdiction
        c. Plaintiff satisfied the requirements for a *quasi in rem* theory since the defendants all held Greyhound stock (Greyhound was a Delaware corporation)
        d. *** Exercises of *quasi in rem* jurisdiction would now satisfy due process only if they met **International Shoe**'s minimum contacts test
        e. *** Shaffer failed the minimum contact test; this is a debatable point
        f. *** Criteria for a proper court
            i. Personal Jurisdiction
                1. Judicial Power
                    A. Due Process Requirement
                    B. State law
                2. Notice
                    A. Due Process Requirement
                    B. Service Requirements
            ii. Subject matter jurisdiction
            iii. Venue
            iv. Joinder
3. **World-Wide Volkswagen v. Woodson**. Forum injury is not enough
    a. Plaintiffs purchased an Audi car from defendant retailer Seaway in New York
    b. Seaway had obtained the car from defendant regional distributor Volkswagen
    c. Plaintiffs were injured when the gas tank of the car exploded during a collision in Oklahoma
    d. Supreme Court held that Oklahoma courts were without minimum contacts necessary to assert personal jurisdiction
    e. Granted, defendants could have foreseen that so mobile a product might reach Oklahoma highways, but "foreseeability" alone has never been a sufficient benchmark for personal jurisdiction under the Due Process Clause
    f. If the only contact with the forum state is that the plaintiff wandered there, there is no personal jurisdiction over the defendant because the burden on the defendant would be enormous
    g. Courts focus on the activity of the seller, rather than the predictable area of use of the product by the buyer
4. **Burger King Corp. v. Rudzewicz**. All of Defendant's Contacts Related to the Controversy Need Not Be With the Forum

a. Through negotiation with Burger King's regional office in Michigan, Rudzewicz and another Michigan defendant obtained a franchise in that state
   b. Defendants failed to make payments, and Burger King brought a federal diversity suit on the franchise agreement in Florida, its headquarters and place of incorporation
   c. Rudzewicz objected to Florida jurisdiction. US Supreme Court ruled in favor of Burger King. There were enough Florida contacts related to the controversy to satisfy the minimum contacts test: Defendants at times dealt directly with Burger King's Miami headquarters, they contracted with BK to have Florida law govern the franchise agreement, and they promised to send their franchise payments to BK's Florida address
   d. Under the circumstances, the Court refused to attach importance to the fact that Rudzewicz had not been in the forum state: "So long as a commercial actor's efforts are *'purposefully directed'* toward residents of another State, we have consistently rejected the notion that an absence of physical contacts can defeat personal jurisdiction there"
   e. To recognize specific jurisdiction only in a place which is the exclusive or *predominant* source of related contacts would often deny forums the legitimate expression of their regulatory interests
5. **Asahi Metal Ind. Co. v. Superior Court**. When Minimum Contacts Are Not Enough
   a. Plaintiff sued in California over an accident that happened there involving the rear tire of his motorcycle.
   b. Defendant Cheng Shin manufactured the tire in Taiwan. It attempted to bring in Asahi, a Japanese concern that manufactured the tire's valve assembly
   c. The US Supreme court ruled that California did not have personal jurisdiction over Asahi
   d. The court used a balancing test of benefits vs. burdens:
      i. Benefit: The interests of the plaintiff and the forum in California's assertion of jurisdiction over Asahi were *slight*
      ii. Burdens: Asahi's burden from defending in California was *severe*
   e. The burden in having to defend away from home will vary depending on how *unfamiliar* or *inconvenient* the forum really is to the defendant. It is probably not oppressive for a defendant to be sued in a state where the defendant conducts highly regularized activities, even if those activities are unrelated to the plaintiff's particular claim (general jurisdiction established)

f. The result in **Asahi** confirmed that minimum contacts between the forum and a nonresident defendant do not guarantee that assertion of personal jurisdiction comports with due process
g. ***Look at who *initiated* the international transaction. If it was the defendant, it will not be hard to show minimum contacts
h. ***A parts manufacturer must *purposefully direct* the product into the stream of commerce, mere awareness is not enough. Purposefully directing is shown by:
    i. Designing the product for the market in the forum state
    ii. Advertising in the forum state
    iii. Establishing channels for providing regular advice to customers in the forum state
    iv. Marketing the product through a distributor who has agreed to serve as the sales agent in the forum state
6. **Burnham v. Superior Court**. The Triumph of Transient Jurisdiction
    a. Transient jurisdiction occurs when a nonresident defendant is actually found and served within the forum state, but when defendant's presence there is:
        i. Only intended to be brief
        ii. Is unrelated to the controversy raised by plaintiff's claim
    b. Transient jurisdiction is a means of circumventing the minimum contacts requirement raised in **International Shoe**
    c. Burnham was served as a defendant in a California divorce action during his brief visit there on business and to visit his children
    d. All the Justices found that California's attempt to exercise transient jurisdiction was permissible, but their reasons differed
    e. Four Justices (Scalia, Rehnquist, Kennedy, White) found it unnecessary to test the case under **International Shoe**; they were willing to uphold transient jurisdiction because it was satisfactory under the old **Pennoyer** doctrine. Moreover, **Shoe** itself used language that implied that minimum contacts were required only if a defendant "be not present within the territory of the forum"
    f. Four other Justices (Marshall, Blackmun, O'Connor, Brennan) applied **Shoe**. Jurisdiction was found sufficient under **Shoe** because Burnham had deliberately partaken (however briefly) of "significant benefits provided by the State". These Justices left open the possibility of a different

result under **Shoe** when defendant's presence in a state is "involuntary or unknowing". See **Grace v. McArthur** where transient jurisdiction was found to exist when defendant was served on an aircraft flying over the airspace of the forum state

k. Notice and Opportunity to be Heard
   i. Federal and state adjudications are binding only when they satisfy the Due Process Clauses of the United States Constitution
   ii. The character of notice will usually depend on the procedure for service of process
      1. Service – the formal means by which process is delivered to a defendant
      2. Process – usually consists of a summons directing defendant to respond or appear in court on penalty of default and a copy of the complaint
   iii. **Mullane v. Central Hanover Bank & Trust Co.**
      1. Beneficiaries fell into three categories
         a. Those whose names and addresses were known. *Must mail process in order to give notice*
         b. Those who were unknowable
         c. Those whose names and addresses could be ascertained at considerable expense
            i. *Constructive notice by publication allowed to the beneficiaries for whom individualized notice was impractical* (b) and (c) above
            ii. Proof of impracticability accompanied by proof of the following will help satisfy due process requirements:
               1. The suit is in the best interest of the absentees
               2. They will be *adequately represented* by one before the court. Adequate representation is a substitute for individual notice
               3. The value of their individual interests is not too great
      2. Rules Regulating Service of Process: The Federal Rule Model
         a. FRCP 4(e) – (j). Plaintiff may mail the complaint, a request for waiver of formal service, and a form explaining the consequences of waiver to the defendant by first class mail
         b. Waiver of service of a summons. FRCP 4(d)
            i. In order to waive, you have to have notice first
            ii. At the option of the defendant
            iii. Deleterious consequences of not waiving:
               1. D has to pay the cost of formal service of process
               2. D doesn't get as long a period to answer the complaint. 20 days v. 60 days

3. If D waives service of a summons, he cannot later file a motion to dismiss for improper service (manner or content)
            c. The procedure is applicable to service outside the state
            d. It imposes on the defendant a duty to avoid unnecessary costs of serving the summons
            e. If there are only a *few* defendants, and notice by mail does not work, then personal service must be done
    l. Long-Arm Statutes. FRCP 4(k)
        i. States were under no obligation to endow their courts with authority for extraterritorial personal jurisdiction. Even when they created extraterritorial jurisdiction, they were free to offer plaintiffs less than the full amount permitted by due process
        ii. They responded by enacting "long-arm" statutes, which provide personal jurisdiction over nonresident defendants who cannot be found and served in the forum state. They have generally taken one of two forms:
            1. The first attempts to categorize factual situations which seem likely to satisfy the minimum contacts test of **International Shoe** and authorizes the court to exercise jurisdiction over nonresidents in such cases, conferring all jurisdiction permitted by state and federal constitutional law. This is used by California
            2. The second does no go up to the limits of due process. The statute will use technical terms that delineate the limits of the state's long arm. Massachusetts uses this form
        iii. The state courts have tended to interpret their statutes to confer all of the jurisdiction permitted by due process, regardless of the statutes' content

VII. VENUE
   a. Rules of venue are rules of convenience for allocating cases territorially, usually among counties within a state and among judicial districts and their divisions within the federal judicial system
   b. Objection to improper venue is waived if not promptly asserted. FRCP 12(h)(1)
   c. Improper venue does not subject a judgment to collateral attack
   d. Most venue statutes are based on some logical relationship between the parties or subject matter of the lawsuit and the place of trial. The following kinds of relationships are typical:
        i. The locus of the property or event that is the subject of the lawsuit
        ii. Where the cause of action arose
        iii. Where the defendant resides, does business, or retains an agent
        iv. Where the plaintiff resides
        v. In suits by or against government parties, where the seat of government is located
   e. The Federal criteria for venue has two general alternatives for venue
        i. The lawsuit can be brought in the judicial district where any defendant resides. 28 USC §1392(a)
            1. The residence of a defendant corporation is "any judicial district in which it is subject to personal jurisdiction at the time the action is

commenced" Both specific and general jurisdiction seem to be implied
2. In multi district states in which the corporation is subject to personal jurisdiction, the corporation is deemed to reside in any district "within which its contacts would be sufficient to subject it to personal jurisdiction if that district were a separate state" 28 USC §1391(c)
  ii. Venue may be found in the judicial district in which a substantial part of the events or omissions giving rise to the claim occurred or a substantial part of the property that is the subject of the action is situated. 28 USC §1391(a)(2) & (b)(2)
  iii. If neither of these venue alternatives is available, the plaintiff has a fallback venue. In diversity-only cases, he may sue "in a judicial district in which the defendants are subject to personal jurisdiction at the time the action commenced." 28 USC 1391(a)(3)
f. Change of Venue
  i. *Transfer* between federal courts
    1. A federal district court may transfer any civil action to any other district or division where it might have been brought. The balance of *convenience* must be heavily in favor of the alternative forum. 28 USC 1404(a)
      a. Transfer between federal courts is better than having a dismissal based on Forum Non Conveniens and then re-filing since there is always some doubt whether the case can be re-filed in another district since there are statute of limitations concerns and the other court may simply refuse to recognize venue
    2. Substitutes for motions to dismiss for lack of venue and personal jurisdiction
      a. The district court of a district in which a case is filed laying venue in the wrong division or district shall dismiss, or if it be in the interest of justice, *transfer* such case to any district or division in which it could have been brought. 28 USC 1406(a)
      b. If a case is filed in a court where there is lack of personal jurisdiction, the court may dismiss or in the interests of justice, transfer the case to a district court where there is personal jurisdiction. The case shall be deemed as if it were filed on the date it was filed in the original court. 28 USC 1631
  ii. Forum Non Conveniens
    1. Sometimes the alternative forum is outside the state's judicial system or even the United States. State courts have no power to transfer cases to the courts of other states, and neither state nor federal courts have the power to transfer cases to the courts of foreign countries. In such cases, most courts permit *dismissal* of

suits under the doctrine of *forum non conveniens*, in anticipation that the plaintiff will recommence the suit in the alternative foreign venue

2. To obtain a *forum non conveniens* dismissal, defendant must satisfy two requirements
    a. First, he must show that an adequate alternative forum is available
        i. **Piper Aircraft Co. v. Reyno**. Plaintiff argued that his case should not be dismissed from a *proper* federal venue under the doctrine of *forum non conveniens* when the alternative Scottish forum would apply less favorable substantive law
        ii. The Supreme Court held that the mere possibility of an unfavorable change in the applicable law does not bar a *forum non conveniens* dismissal, unless the change makes the remedy "so clearly inadequate or unsatisfactory that it is no remedy at all"
        iii. On the other hand, a lack of jurisdiction in the alternative forum clearly renders it inadequate for *forum non conveniens* purposes
    b. Second, the defendant must show that considerations of party and forum *convenience* override the plaintiff's choice of forum and justify dismissal
        i. Typical party or private considerations include
            1. Relative ease of access to proof
            2. Availability of compulsory process for attendance of witnesses and the cost of obtaining their attendance
            3. The possibility of obtaining a jury view the scene of the accident or property which is the subject of the action
            4. The enforceability of any eventual judgment in the original forum
        ii. If the above factors indicate that the alternative forum would be more convenient for the parties, then the plaintiff's choice of forum was presumably tactical, or even harassing, and may therefore be disturbed
        iii. Forum or public considerations reflect chiefly the relative benefits and burdens of imposing litigation on the contending forums
            1. Effect on judicial calendars
            2. Imposition of jury duty on the forum community
            3. Local interest in the controversy
            4. Choice of law

A. The public interest is best served by localizing the litigation, and assigning it to the forum most familiar with the applicable law

VIII. **SUBJECT MATTER JURISDICTION**
   a. Subject matter jurisdiction refers to a court's power or "competence" to decide a particular kind of controversy
   b. To render a binding decision, the court must be "competent by its constitution", i.e., by the law of its creation
   c. Typically that law will include the constitution of the sovereign + legislation + common law interpretation of such legislation by the courts
   d. Subject matter jurisdiction can be concurrent – shared between several different kinds of courts, or exclusive – restricted to a particular kind of court
      i. State courts of general jurisdiction and federal district courts have concurrent jurisdiction of most cases involving questions of federal constitutional or statutory law
   e. Parties cannot enlarge a federal court's subject matter jurisdiction by consent or waiver
   f. Parties may challenge a federal court's subject matter jurisdiction at any point in the litigation, including appeal
      i. Collateral attacks on subject matter jurisdiction – challenges made not at trial or on direct appeal but in a separate litigation, are not allowed except in extraordinary circumstances
   g. A federal court is required on its own motion to consider whether it has subject matter jurisdiction when the litigants have not raised the question. FRCP 12(h)(3)
   h. Subject matter jurisdiction of the federal courts
      i. The United States Constitution sets out the permissible scope of the judicial power of federal courts in Article III, § 2.
         1. Cases "*arising under* this Constitution, the Laws of the United States, and Treaties made…under their Authority," popularly knows as *federal question* jurisdiction
         2. Cases between citizens of different states, popularly known as *diversity* jurisdiction
      ii. Article III directly vests the Supreme Court with original jurisdiction of cases
      iii. In contrast, Article III vests no jurisdiction in lower federal courts. Instead it authorizes Congress to create and endow them with subject matter jurisdiction
      iv. ***Congress therefore has the constitutional authority to decide by legislation how much of the federal subject matter jurisdiction available under Article III shall be vested in the lower federal courts
   i. Federal Question Jurisdiction
      i. Constitutional scope – Federal jurisdiction is broadly given to the supreme court
      ii. Statutory scope – The courts have given a narrow scope to statutory federal question jurisdiction

1. Ask these two questions. If both are satisfied, there will be subject matter jurisdiction. If only one is satisfied, there *may* be subject matter jurisdiction:
   a. Does federal law create the cause of action? Ex: A Civil Rights statute giving you the right to sue
   b. Does federal law identify the elements of the plaintiff's claim?
2. However, many of the cases are treated in a pragmatic way:
   a. Does the case need a sympathetic federal court?
   b. Will the case erode the distinctive character of the state court? Will it overburden the federal court?
        iii. The well-pleaded complaint rule. **Louisville & Nashville R.R. v. Mottley**. It is not enough that there is a *potential* federal question in a case, it must appear in plaintiff's well-pleaded complaint
j. Diversity Jurisdiciton
     i. Listed under 28 USC §1332
    ii. The *Erie* doctrine requires federal courts sitting in diversity to apply state law as rules of decision
   iii. The courts are barred by statute from asserting jurisdiction when a party contrives to create diversity
   iv. Diversity Jurisdiction has two levels of analysis
       1. Constitutional: Article III, § 2 gives broad diversity jurisdiction (minimal diversity) as long as the parties to the lawsuit are each from different states
       2. Statutory: 28 USC §1332 gives narrow diversity jurisdiction (complete diversity). If any party to the lawsuit is from the same state, there is no diversity jurisdiction. The matter in controversy has to be greater than 75k.
    v. Citizenship
       1. The courts look to the citizenship of the parties at the commencement of the action
       2. Citizenship for diversity purposes requires a party to be both a citizen of the Unites States and of a state
       3. Citizenship=domicile. Domicile is established by the concurrent establishment of a physical residence in a state and an intent to remain there indefinitely
          a. Intent can only be shown circumstantially, e.g., driver's license, residence, etc.
       4. An American citizen domiciled abroad is a citizen of every state, therefore there is no diversity jurisdiction
   vi. Amount in controversy. Must exceed $75,000. Courts liberally interpret this requirement. Only dismiss the case if the court can do so with *legal certainty*
  vii. Aggregating multiple claims
       1. A plaintiff may aggregate all the claims he asserts against a single defendant, whether or not they are transactionally related and whether or not any of them alone satisfies the jurisdictional amount

2. When there are multiple plaintiffs and defendants, aggregation is allowed if the parties have a common undivided interest or title
   k. Removal Jurisdiction
      i. Removal jurisdiction is an exception to the rule that the plaintiff chooses the court
      ii. A defendant may pursuant to USC 28 §1441 remove a civil action from a state court with personal jurisdiction to federal court
      iii. The purpose of removal is to make the option of suit in federal court as available to defendants (except for resident defendants in a diversity-only case) as it is to plaintiffs
      iv. Removal is a protective option for defendants only. A plaintiff who is sued upon a federal counterclaim cannot remove
      v. Removal is intended just to make existing federal jurisdiction available to defendants. Removal jurisdiction is therefore keyed to original jurisdiction
      vi. 28 USC §1359. Cannot manufacture federal jurisdiction by joining a false party to your claim
      vii. An in-stater cannot remove on the basis of diversity jurisdiction if the out of stater sues in state
   l. Supplemental Jurisdiction
      i. 28 USC § 1367 governs
      ii. 1367 (a): Need common nucleus (logical relationship between the claims) + substantial federal claim
      iii. 1367 (b): The main claim must be based on federal law, NOT based on diversity
      iv. 1367 (c): Discretion of judge on considerations of judicial economy, convenience, and fairness to litigants

IX. STATE LAW IN FEDERAL COURTS "ERIE DOCTRINE"
   a. **Erie R.R. co. v. Tompkins**. In *diversity cases* the federal court should apply the substantive law of the state in which the court is located
   b. Twin aims of Erie
      i. To avoid inequitable administration of laws, i.e., different treatment of cases in state court and in federal court based on diversity
      ii. To discourage forum shopping
         1. Good reason: to get to a federal court if you feel that you would be discriminated against in some way by the state court
         2. Bad reason: you want to get a favorable federal decision not backed up by congress. This erodes state power. Ex: **Black and White Taxicab**
   c. Substance versus Procedure
      i. Erie requires that a distinction be made between substantive and procedural rules. If a rule is deemed to be substantive, the forum state law applies. If the rule is procedural, the federal law applies. However, problems arise in determining whether something can be classified either as procedural or substantive
      ii. The substantive/procedural distinction is based on an *outcome-determinative test*: if application of the federal rule (e.g. statute of

limitations) would produce a different outcome, i.e., lead to forum shopping, than that which would occur if the action were brought in state court, then the federal courts must follow the state rule, so that a different result would not occur solely because the case was based in a federal court. **Guaranty Trust Co. v. York**

  iii. In matters essential to the independence of the federal court (e.g., judge-jury relationships), when the conflicting state rule is not an integral part of the state-created substantive rights and duties involved in the action, the federal rule controls. **Byrd v. Blue Ridge Rural Electric Co-op Inc. Byrd** introduces a *balancing test* that requires weighing the policies underlying the respective federal and state rules; the result might have been different if the policy interests of the federal courts had been weaker, or those of the state stronger

  iv. The 7th Amendment is interpreted such that review of jury decisions is allowed under the common law since it is dynamic. The federal statute in question is wholly judge-made, and it would encourage forum shopping, so the state law applies. **Gasperini v. Center for Humanities**

  v. Rules of Decision Act, 28 USC § 1652 governs, this rule implies that until Congress acts in an area of concurrent state power by passing a *statute*, state law governs. Advocates of expanded federal power have the burden of getting Congress to act clearly. When a statute is passed by Congress, the states have consented to it because Congress is composed of representatives from all the states

  vi. "Substantive". If the focus of the law is out of court, then it is substantive. If the focus of the law is in court, then it is procedural

 d. FRCP. **Hanna v. Plummer**
  i. The FRCP represent expressions of federal policy and are legitimate exercises of federal power under Article I, §8 and Article III, §1 of the Constitution
   1. Article I, §8 – Commerce clause; congress shall have power to regulate commerce among the several states. Congress can make laws which are necessary and proper for carrying into execution the above power
   2. Article III, §1 – The judicial Power of the United States shall be vested in on supreme court, and in such inferior Courts as the Congress may from time to time ordain and establish
  ii. Matters expressly covered by the FRCP are *presumptively* procedural and need not yield to state rules. The court interprets the FRCP in question narrowly so that it doesn't speak to the issue at hand, thereby avoiding confrontation with state law
  iii. Warren's view:
   1. Narrowly interpret the FRCP
   2. Judge the FRCP to be valid if it can rationally be classified as procedural

 e. FRCP. **Ragan v. Merchants Transfer Co.** (Academic Analysis)

i. FRCP can displace state practices to the contrary even when the application of state practice would lead to a different result. However, the *FRCP cannot abridge, enlarge, or modify a substantive state right*. <u>28 USC §2072(b)</u> (Rules Enabling Act)
   ii. A defendant's right to repose is a substantive right. The FRCP would abridge it, so state law governs
   iii. A federal rule is not the same as a statute
f. Rules of Evidence. The Federal Rules of Evidence control over conflicting state rules in an action in federal court
g. Special Federal Common Law
   i. Can be changed by congress
   ii. Narrow scope
   iii. Federal courts are free to develop federal common law only on matters of substantial national concern that fall within the powers given the federal government by the Constitution
h. ***** EXAM APPROACH *****

   1. Is the federal law involved based on a statute, FRCP, The Constitution (interpreted by special federal common law), or wholly judge-made federal law?
      a. If federal law is based on a *statute, FRCP*, or *The Constitution* ask:
         i. Does the statute, FRCP, or Constitution apply, i.e., is it broad enough to cover the issue presented?
            1. If yes – federal law applies (outcome determinative test does not apply)
               A. If a FRCP is in question, ask: Does the FRCP affect a state's substantive right?
                  i. Yes – state law applies
                  ii. No – FRCP applies
            2. If no – state law applies
      b. If a *wholly judge-made federal law* is involved and applicable to the issue presented, ask:
         i. Will application of the federal practice undermine the "twin aims" of Erie, i.e., encourage forum shopping and result in discrimination because there may be a different result in a case brought in federal rather than state court? In answering the question consider and balance the state and federal interests at stake (outcome determinative test)
            1. If yes – state law applies
            2. If no – the federal practice applies

X. PRECLUSION: CLAIM PRECLUSION
a. Declaratory judgments v. Judgments

i. A declaratory judgment is one in which the court declares the rights or legal relations of the parties instead of awarding affirmative relief
ii. A judgment is defined as any final order or final decree fully disposing of the case
b. Claim Preclusion (*Res Judicata*) = Mandatory joinder of claims.
   i. The doctrines of bar and merger prescribe the effect of a judgment on the cause of action involved. The general rule is that the parties are precluded from relitigating the **same cause of action** or from splitting a cause of action
   ii. Cause of Action. Whether a second suit involves the same cause of action may be determined by a variety of tests. These tests are:
      1. Same Transaction or Occurrence (Federal Courts and most states)
         a. If the second action arises out of the same transaction or occurrence, then it will be subject to claim preclusion
            i. Ex: Sully is injured when a truck causes him to swerve his car off the road and wrap it around a telephone pole. Sully's claims for personal injury and for damage to the auto must be asserted together since they both arise out of the same accident
        b. FRCP 13(a) – If a **defendant** has a cause of action that arises out of the same transaction or occurrence, he must assert it in the 1st action
      2. Same Cause of Action (Narrow traditional view)
         a. If the same evidence will support both actions, then the same cause of action is involved
            i. Ex: The same evidence test would apply to personal injury and property damage claims arising out of a single tort
         b. Different claims could arise out of the same transaction or occurrence, but they won't be precluded since the core set of operative facts for each is different
c. Requirements
   i. Claim Preclusion will apply only if the first action ended in a **final judgment on the merits**. See **Saylor v. Lindsley.** Thus, it will not apply to interlocutory orders or to dismissals for lack of jurisdiction or venue FRCP 41(b). However, most jurisdictions give claim preclusion effect to a default judgment even though there has been no adversarial adjudication. A pre-trial dismissal also will be given claim preclusion effect when it is with prejudice, but not when it is without prejudice
d. Merger
   i. Merger applies when the *prevailing* party in one action seeks to assert the *same cause of action* in another suit against the same party. The second claim is said to "merge" into the judgment on the first claim

                1. Ex: Shawn sues Jeff on a negligence claim arising from a car accident for personal injuries. Shawn wins. Shawn cannot sue Jeff in a second suit for damage to the car caused by the same accident
    e. Bar
        i. Bar applies when an unsuccessful claimant in one action attempts to relitigate the same cause of action in a subsequent suit against the same party. The second claim is said to be "barred" by the judgment on the first
            1. Ex: Ramon sues Matty Z on a negligence claim arising from a car accident for personal injuries. Ramon loses. Ramon cannot sue Matty Z in a second suit for damage to the car caused by the same accident
    f. Could have been joined in first action
    g. Privity
        i. Need privity on both sides
        ii. If there are doubts about privity, will resolve against granting privity
XI. **PRECLUSION: ISSUE PRECLUSION**
    a. The doctrine of issue preclusion (collateral estoppel) prohibits the relitigation of a fact issue that was previously adjudicated on the merits. Thus, the doctrine relates to **issues** as opposed to whole claims and may apply even though a **separate cause of action** is being litigated between the same parties
    b. Prerequisites. There are three basic requirements to a finding that an issue is collaterally estopped. They are
        i. Identical Issue
            1. The issue of fact in the second action must be identical to the issue in the first action and must arise from the same set of circumstances to be precluded. **Make certain the burden of proof is the same in both actions**, which would not be true if one action is civil (preponderance of evidence) and the other criminal (beyond a reasonable doubt)
        ii. Final Judgment (not necessarily on merits)
        iii. Actually Decided
            1. There must be an absolute certainty that the issue in the first action actually was decided. Thus, if the holding is ambiguous as to the decision on certain issues, then issue preclusion cannot be invoked on those issues
                a. Ex: If Chris S. sues Derek O. for negligence and Derek counterclaims for contributory negligence and there is a judgment for Derek, that judgment could have resulted either because Derek was found to be free from negligence or because Chris was found to be contributorily negligent, or both. It is not clear on which ground the judgment rests, so neither issue would be precluded
        iv. Issue Absolutely Necessary
            1. Any issue to which a party is attempting to apply issue preclusion must have been **absolutely necessary to the first action**, since if

the issue was necessary, then the court can be certain that it was actually litigated
c. Persons and Bound – General Rule
    i. Claim preclusion can only operate against someone who was a party in the first action. Everyone "gets his day in court". Traditionally, the availability of claim preclusion was further limited by a **mutuality** requirement
    ii. Ex: Sully, Selden, and Ohly are in a car with Ohly driving. They get in an accident with another car driven by Lennox. Ohly sues Lennox for negligence, and Lennox counterclaims. Lennox wins. Sully sues both Ohly and Lennox for personal injuries due to their negligence. Lennox moves to dismiss on the ground that Sully is issue precluded from relitigation of Lennox's negligence. The motion should be denied since issue preclusion cannot be asserted against a non-party and Sully had no opportunity to litigate the issue of Lennox's negligence in the first action
    iii. Privity. A person who is not a party to an action still may find himself bound by a judgment in the action, whether favorable or not, if he is in privity with a party. The legal definition of a person in privity with another is a person so identified in interest with another that he represents the same legal right. Need privity at least on the losing side.
    iv. Mutuality
        1. The mutuality doctrine **prevented** a person from using a judgment to bar the relitigation of an issue in a subsequent suit if his opponent could not have used the judgment against him if it had been decided the other way. Because a judgment could not be asserted against a non-party, that non-party could not use that judgment in a subsequent action
        2. Breakdown in Mutuality is the modern rule. In many states now, a person who was **not** a party to the first lawsuit may be allowed to issue preclude relitigation of an issue in a second lawsuit by a party in the first action. However, some jurisdictions only permit use of issue preclusion by a non-party defensively or offensively
        3. Defensive Issue Preclusion
            a. All jurisdictions that have abandoned the mutuality doctrine permit defensive use of issue preclusion, in part because it operates to prevent repeated litigation of the same factual issue
                i. Ex: As a result of a two-car accident, Aaron, a passenger in one of the cars, sues Bobby, the driver of the second car, alleging negligence. Aaron wins on a jury finding that Bobby was negligent. Then Bobby sues Cooper, the driver of the first car. Cooper asserts that Bobby is contributorily negligent and is issue precluded from denying that he (Bobby) is negligent, based on the verdict in the first action between Aaron and Bobby

4. Offensive Issue Preclusion
    a. Only a few jurisdictions permit offensive use of issue preclusion by a non-party in the first action to support a claim because it can operate to encourage multiple litigation. In those jurisdictions, moreover, the court has the **discretion** to deny an offensive use
        i. Ex: As a result of a two-car accident, Aaron, a passenger in one of the cars, sues Bobby, the driver of the second car, alleging negligence. Aaron wins on a jury finding that Bobby was negligent. Then Cooper, the driver of the first car, sues Bobby. Cooper asserts that Bobby is contributorily negligent and is issue precluded from denying that he (Bobby) is negligent, based on the verdict in the first action between Aaron and Bobby. In some jurisdictions, this offensive use of issue preclusion may be permitted in the court's discretion as long as Bobby had **an opportunity and incentive to litigate the issue in the first action**
    b. Factors guiding discretion
        i. Whether the person asserting issue preclusion could easily have joined in the first action
        ii. Whether the offensive use is fair to the defendant
            1. Did defendant have little incentive ot defend 1st action vigorously
            2. 2nd action gives procedural opportunities to defendant not available in1st
            3. This fairness requirement CANNOT be met when there are opposing judgments

END

About The Author

Kevin Lomax, JD graduated from a top three undergraduate school and then attended a top ten law school, where he graduated near the top of his class. Kevin is not the author's real name, as he wishes to stay anonymous at his current place of employment. Kevin suggests that you watch movies such as *The Firm* and *The Devil's Advocate* because these movies only hint at the "fun" that will await you in big law life upon graduating from law school.